D1716107

Extinct Monsters

# Giant Kangaroo

by Carol K. Lindeen

Reading Consultant:
Barbara J. Fox
Reading Specialist
North Carolina State University

Content Consultant:
Dr. Richard Gillespie
Visiting Fellow, Department of Archaeology and Natural History
Australian National University, Canberra

Capstone
press

Mankato, Minnesota

Blazers is published by Capstone Press,
151 Good Counsel Drive, P.O. Box 669, Mankato, Minnesota 56002.
www.capstonepress.com

Library of Congress Cataloging-in-Publication Data
Lindeen, Carol, 1976–
    Giant kangaroo / by Carol K. Lindeen.
    p. cm.—(Blazers. Extinct monsters)
    Summary: "Simple text and illustrations describe giant kangaroos, how they
lived, and how they became extinct"—Provided by publisher.
    Includes bibliographical references and index.
    ISBN-13: 978-1-4296-0114-6 (hardcover)
    ISBN-10: 1-4296-0114-0 (hardcover)
    1. Procoptodon—Juvenile literature. 2. Extinct animals—Juvenile literature.
I. Title. II. Series.
QE882.M34L56 2008
599.2'2—dc22                                                    2006037263

**Editorial Credits**
Jenny Marks, editor; Ted Williams, designer; Jon Hughes and
    Russell Gooday/www.pixelshack.com, illustrators;
    Wanda Winch, photo researcher

**Photo Credits**
Flinders University of South Australia/Rod Wells, 29 (skull)
Shutterstock/EcoPrint, 22–23 (grassy landscape); Michael Fuery, 20–21
    (Australian grasses), 26–27 (Australian landscape); Richard Sak,
    cover (Australian grass)

1  2  3  4  5  6  12  11  10  09  08  07

# Australia Long Ago

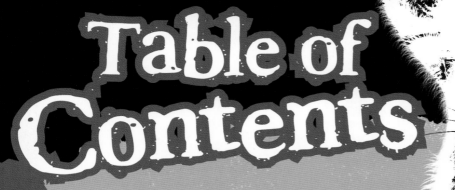

# Table of Contents

A million years ago, Australia was a wild, wooded land. Enormous animals roamed the forests and plains.

One monstrous animal grew five times as large as today's kangaroos. The Procoptodon goliah (pro-COP-tuh-don goh-LYE-uh) was a huge, leaping beast.

# Monster Fact

Giant kangaroos and other huge animals that lived long ago are called megafauna.

# Hooks and Hooves

The giant kangaroo stood about 10 feet (3 meters) tall and weighed about 500 pounds (227 kilograms). Its short, flat face had strong jaws and teeth.

The giant kangaroo had long, muscled arms that reached high above its head. The kangaroo used its arms like crutches when it walked.

11

Giant kangaroos had hooklike claws on each finger. The long, sharp claws helped kangaroos rip grass and leaves to eat.

# Monster Fact

*Like kangaroos today, the giant kangaroo carried its young in a pouch on its belly.*

14

Giant kangaroos had long feet with one strong toe. Hooflike claws gave kangaroos extra jumping power.

# Jumping and Reaching

When in danger, the giant
kangaroos' best defense
was speed. Their powerful
legs bounced them away
from attackers.

Giant kangaroos kept a careful watch for predators. Giant ripper lizards could make a meal out of a kangaroo.

# Monster Fact

*Giant kangaroos' top speed was around 30 miles (48 kilometers) per hour.*

19

If it was safe to eat, a kangaroo stood on its toes and balanced with its tail. On tiptoe, this giant reached even higher to tear leaves off tall trees.

# The End of a Giant

Humans came to Australia
about 45,000 years ago.
People hunted the animals,
including giant kangaroos.

Humans built fires that burned plants the kangaroos ate. Fewer and fewer giant kangaroos could survive.

By about 40,000 years ago, the giant kangaroo was extinct. This weird beast would leap across the land no more.

# Monster Fact

The banded hare-wallaby is the giant kangaroo's closest living relative. This harelike marsupial weighs 4 pounds (1.8 kilograms).

Fossils are all that is left of the giant kangaroo. Scientists find remains of this big beast across Australia.

# Monster Fact

*Many giant kangaroo fossils were found in Australia's Naracoorte Caves. The animals fell into pits and couldn't climb out.*

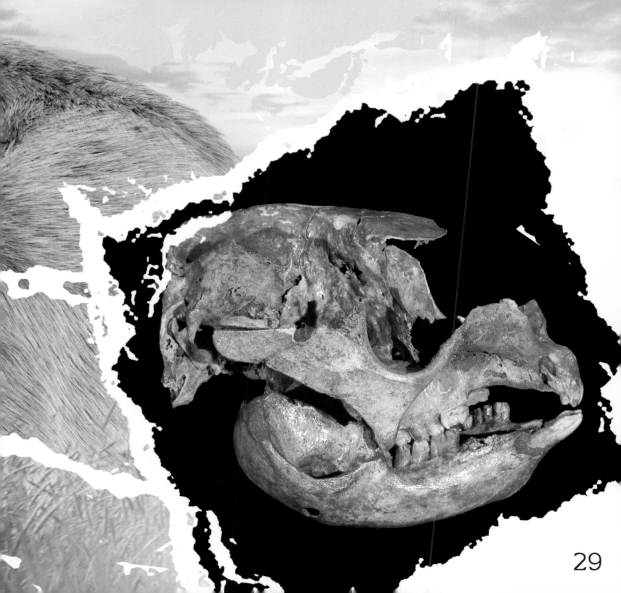

29

# Glossary

**defense** (di-FENSS)—a way to protect someone or something from an attack

**enormous** (i-NOR-muhss)—extremely large

**extinct** (ek-STINGKT)—no longer living; an extinct animal is one that has died out, with no more of its kind.

**fossil** (FOSS-uhl)—the remains or a trace of an animal or plant preserved in rock or in the earth

**marsupial** (mar-SOO-pee-uhl)—an animal that carries its young in a pouch

**megafauna** (MEG-uh-FAWN-uh)—large animals that lived around the time of the Ice Age

**monstrous** (MON-struss)—large and frightening

**plain** (PLANE)—a large, flat area of land

**predator** (PRED-uh-tur)—an animal that hunts other animals for food

**survive** (sur-VIVE)—to continue to live

**weird** (WIHRD)—strange or mysterious

# Read More

Gunzi, Christiane. *The Best Book of Endangered and Extinct Animals.* Boston: Kingfisher, 2004.

Jay, Michael. *Ice Age Beasts.* Prehistoric Animals. Chicago: Raintree, 2004.

Turner, Alan. *National Geographic Prehistoric Mammals.* Washington, D.C.: National Geographic, 2004.

# Internet Sites

FactHound offers a safe, fun way to find Internet sites related to this book. All of the sites on FactHound have been researched by our staff.

Here's how:
1. Visit *www.facthound.com*
2. Choose your grade level.
3. Type in this book ID **1429601140** for age-appropriate sites. You may also browse subjects by clicking on letters, or by clicking on pictures and words.
4. Click on the **Fetch It** button.

**FactHound will fetch the best sites for you!**

# Index